Book 11

Dad and Sam

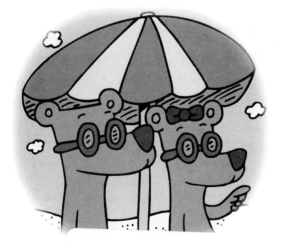

b
Illustra  riani

SCHOLASTIC

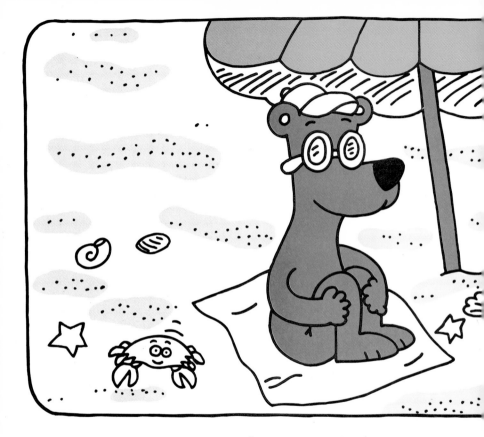

Dad sat.

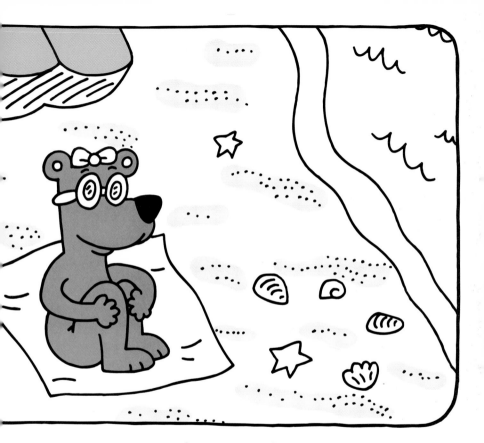

Sam sat.

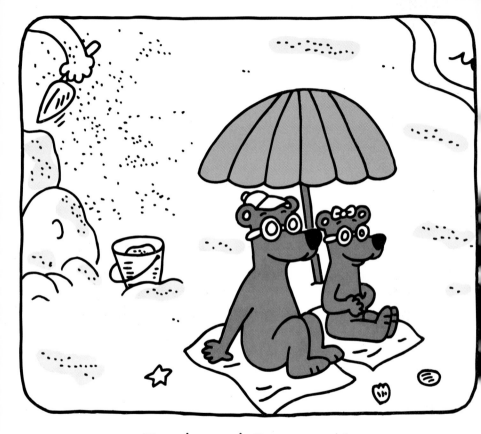

Dad and Sam sat.

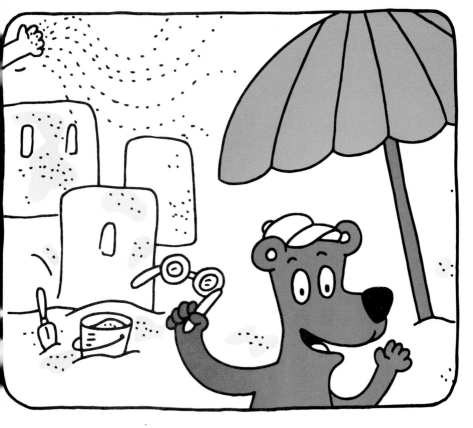

Dad said, "I like to see the sand."

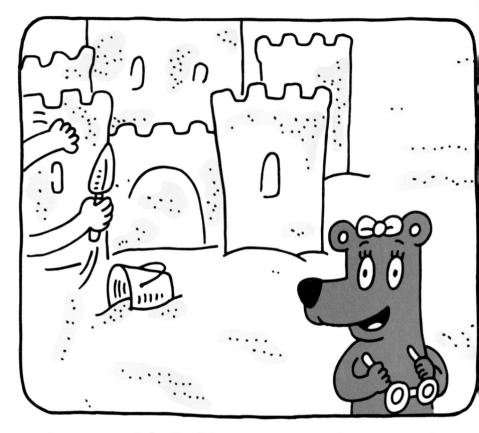

Sam said, "I like to see the sand."

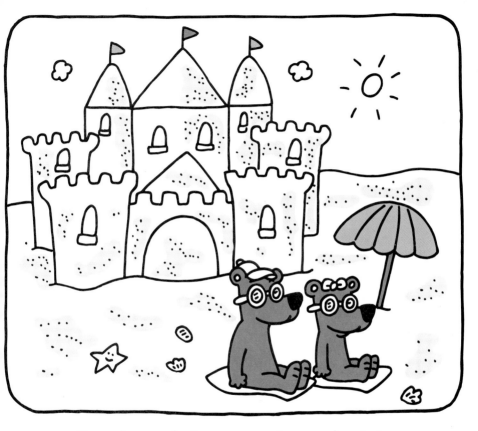

Dad and Sam sat and sat.

My Words

*said

Ss
Sam
sand

-at
sat

*new high frequency words